Strength in the Dark

Coreena Schmitz

Strength in the Dark © 2022 Coreena
Schmitz

All rights reserved.

Coreena Schmitz asserts the moral right to
be identified as author of this work.

Presentation by *BookLeaf Publishing*

Web: www.bookleafpub.com

E-mail: info@bookleafpub.com

ISBN: 978-93-95950-64-0

First edition 2022

DEDICATION

I would like to dedicate this book to my daughters, Casey and Jessica. They have been my reason for living. They helped me grow and become the person I am today. I would also like to thank my husband, Justin, for being my rock. You have supported me in making this dream come true. I also want to dedicate this book to my late mother, Cindy. She was strong no matter what she went through she never gave up. I know you are watching over me now. I hope I made you proud.

ACKNOWLEDGEMENT

I would like to thank Bookleaf Publishing for giving me the chance to share my words with others. I would like to thank my daughter, Jessica for helping me get my poems together so I can share them all with you.

PREFACE

The poems in this book were written to express my thoughts and feelings when the words would not come out. As a teenager, life can be harsh and these poems are my thoughts when I was struggling with bullying, abuse, and abandonment.

Other poems are about the good times when my daughters were born. About friends that have always been there when I needed them and love. We all need to feel love in our lives to help us grow and become our best selves.

My hope for this book is to help others with their own voices. I know how hard it can be to express how we feel. I want to help others learn ways to express themselves.

Some Day

I've been run over
stepped on
Broken and cracked
But I always come back

Some day that will change

Until then I'll wait for you
I can love no one else
My heart and mind
It will take time to heal
When you get back
Maybe we make a deal
And I'll tell you how I fell

When you get here
Let me know what you think
No matter what you say
Hey, I want you to know
There's a place in my heart
Where your memory will stay with me
until my heart stops beating and takes my last
breath

Live or Die

If I could fly
I'd jump out the window
And see how high
I could fly
I wouldn't be scared
Even if I die
I only wanna try

Jump if you wanna live
Jump if you wanna die

Heaven or hell
That's not swell
If there were only
Someone I could tell

Jump if you wanna live
Jump if you wanna die

SPLAT
How could I?
Why would I?

The day I could fly
I changed my life

I used a knife
killed my soul
Dug a hole
As I fold

That night I could only cry
Understand?
I only try
so why do I lie
I just wanna die

Jump if you wanna live
Jump if you wanna die

Now my time is here
I have no fear
and now I cry
My last tear
For my very last year
is drawing near

Jump if you wanna live
Jump if you wanna die

My life is at it's end
And has been

Angel

Your call above
came to fast
We cried our tears
To no end

Unwilling to accept
The truth and facts
That you have gone
Never to come back

Though it hurts to say goodbye
We know you're free
Flying in the sky
with the wings of an angel
by our sides

My Hope

You dried my tears
you mended my scars

No days are easy
But with you
It's a little less hard

Your hazel eyes
so handsome and kind
It makes my heart flutter
every single time

As we grow old
I'll stay by your side
Through the thick and thin
Through love and strife

You are my soul
Always my mate
Together forever
we will always stay

The Key

I was walking along the lakeside
I found a key washed in from the tide

It was little, it was small
It was a key, but that's not all

The key was old, it was tarnished in gold

It unlocked dreams
from a faraway land

That's not all, I am told
the time stands still
there the stars are sold

Your soul lives on
when you grow old
it's like, life after death

Then the key washes away to another seaside

Sound of the Wind

As winds tell tales
speak with such devotion
To the one whose heart runs wild
The one whose eyes speak
A tale that only they can understand
yet are the tales we speak
okay to leave our tongues

Looking a mess
would anyone hire me
can't you see
I wear no shoes and have little to eat
Don't my eyes show enough
To tell you the secrets in which we live by

Don't you see,
wrapped up in greed and money,
That I am human too

My Dream of Love

Love is hard
When you love
Twice as much
Be on guard

The winds whispering touch
as it roams your body
saying softly
The words of romance

Your body swaying
as if to dance
this dream I dream of love
soaring like a dove

High and above
Then you wake up
was it the dream of passion
or forgotten pride

My, oh my
this dream I dream
will it last?

The Prison

This house is like a prison
The floors creaking
with every step I take
the sinks are leaking

BAAM

you can hear the doors slam

CLICK

the doors have locked me in
the lights are blinking
the clock is ticking

tick....tock...tick....tock

Friends Forever

Friends fall apart
going on with life
forgetting those fun times

Then suddenly they appear
with stories of the past years
describing the men and children
in their lives

I wonder if we will be the friends
we were before
As much as I wish
only time will tell

These times apart
how have they been?
Do you remember the times in
the past?
The things we have been through together

Unbelievable that so much
has gone by
we graduated
I gave birth to twin girls
I have been engaged for 2 years

You are due in November
you have a man
And so much more has happened

Friends grow apart
going on with life
but they never forget someone
That was always there

Don't Belong

It's not my place
It's not my home
It's not my family
Even if I hoped
I'm extra baggage
That they don't need
weighing down
Their whole family
What's my purpose?
Why am I here?
I'm the child
No one holds dear
The one that's not loved
And always forgotten
I am just the one
That will never belong

No Where To Go

Alone at night
No place to go
My hope is gone
My faith is blown
The darkness surrounds me
it swallows me whole
Where do I go?
Which way to turn
I hear a voice
Small yet clear
Do I follow
or stay here?
I take a step
Then two then three
Walking forward
I spot a light
A little thing
That shines so bright
Reaching out
I yearn to touch
Only for the light
To disappear furthermore

Never There

When I was crying
When I was sad
When my heart
was hurting so bad
I hoped to see you
To see your face
To feel happiness
and be at peace
but you weren't there
you never are
Saying you'll be here
in my moment of need
But never showing up
Leading me to
a false hope

Blue

Blue is like the sky over you
or like the sparkling ocean, blue

Blue is the color of some eyes
As you stare deep into mine

Blue is like bluebirds
singing in the tree and flying free

Blue is the color for you and me

Empty

My heart has been broken
so many times
Twice would have been nice
But five is too many

They take a piece of my heart as a token
Finally, my feelings have spoken

Don't play with my heart
If it wasn't meant to be
Tell me
Don't lead me on
I don't cost very much
There is no fee

I just expect you to love me
He's in my thoughts and dreams
And memories
But my life is empty without, he

Love

Petals float
feelings grow
under the tree
where lovers go

They spend their days
and spend their nights
holding each other
through their lives

In the dark
They always fight
To keep
the other one alight

No matter how big
No matter how far
Together forever
Never to part

Not Worthy

You love me so much
As you always say
And support me
Through everything
The big and the small
The bad and the good
You are a queen
So precious and sweet
Though sometimes I worry
That I am not worthy
To be in your presence
Full of glory
And though I feel I'm not worthy
I'll always be there
To hug and hold you
And always support you
And give you my heart
That holds all my love

Dying

My mom is dying
it makes me want to start crying
now I'm lying

I don't have any more tears to shed
I just feel like dying
inside I think of ways to keep trying

I can't live without her
Please help me, Sir
When I look at her
I wish it was me not her
I want her pain to be mine
Please tell me, She'll be fine

Why does she have to go through this
She never did anything wrong
to die, a slow painful death

You

Since I met you...
I'm alive
I'm free
untouchable to anyone, but you
You trust me
I trust you
I care for you
You love me inside and out
I've never felt this way before
My heart keeps begging for more
There is passion
There is pain
Deep down inside
there's a hold I have never felt before
I count the hours I spend with you
Your sweet
between us there is heat
Your sensitive
and an understanding man
Your patient
Your honest
You're the man of my dreams
So far the only dream that has come true

The Day of Pain

September 11th
the day that changes us all
from country to country
we heard a cry

As the planes crashed
the buildings fall
the destruction unbearable
people screaming, people dying

I cry as they fall
from the sky
I ask, why us? What did we do?

People running to dodge death
tears streaming down sooty faces
screams of terror are heard throughout
the poor and wealthy come together
we pray for the lost
and hope they are now in a better place

September 11th
A day I pray we will never forget
A day of pain and heartache

My Angels

I remember the day you were born......
The silence before the first breathe of life
The shrill screams piercing the air
as my first little girl was put upon my chest

A minute later a second scream
could be heard throughout the halls
as my second angel was born

Two beings that were so tiny and fragile
crying to hear the sound
of momma's soft voice
Soothing them as they open their eyes
for the first time

They look like their mother no doubt
and will be stars in their daddy's eyes

There are no words that came to mind
As they looked up at me
I became lost within their gassy smiles
and large blue eyes

I knew then no matter what the cost
they would always be the loves of my life

Change

Life is hard
It gets in the way
but you make the choice
To make a change
To start a new

No hate no lies
No pills no fights
Just faith and life
So ask yourself.....

Do I let them break me?
Do I take the fall?
or do I get up?
Stand tall

And change my future
once and for all